Little Dinosaurs Spot-the-Differences Activity Book

Fran Newman-D'Amico

DOVER PUBLICATIONS, INC.
Mineola, New York

Bibliographical Note

Little Dinosaurs Spot-the-Differences Activity Book is a new
work, first published by Dover Publications, Inc., in 2001.

International Standard Book Number
ISBN-13: 978-0-486-41613-7
ISBN-10: 0-486-41613-5

Manufactured in the United States by Courier Corporation
41613505
www.doverpublications.com

NOTE

In this little activity book, you will see many of the dinosaurs that lived millions of years ago. They come from all three periods of dinosaur history—Triassic (try-YASS-ick), Jurassic (ju-RASS-ick), and Cretaceous (kri-TAY-shis). Of course, none of them is alive today. What we know about dinosaurs comes from our study of their bones, which have been found all over the planet. In this book, each dinosaur is shown in two pictures. The second picture has changes that make it different from the first. Look carefully and find these differences. Try to do all of the pages on your own before you look at the Solutions, which begin on page 58. You can enjoy coloring in the pictures as well. Have fun!

This picture of Procompsognathus
(PRO-komp-so-NAYTH-us) looks like the
picture on the opposite page, doesn't it?

4

But this picture is different—4 things have changed.
Find and circle the 4 things.

Here is Anatosaurus (an-at-oh-SORE-us)
getting ready to eat a juicy plant.

What 5 things are different in this picture?
Find and circle them.

Ankylosaurus (an-KEY-low-SORE-us)
lived in parts of North America.

Now look at this picture. Find and circle
the 5 things that are different.

Staurikosaurus (store-IK-oh-SORE-us)
was a small dinosaur, only about 6 feet long.

Four things are different in this picture.
Circle them as you find them.

11

The name Triceratops (try-SER-uh-tops)
means "three-horned face." You can see why!

Here is the same picture, but 6 things
have changed. Find and circle them.

13

Like many dinosaurs, Maiasura (MY-ah-SORE-ah)
walked on its two back legs.

Here is Maiasura, but now 4 things are different.
Find and circle these changes.

The small Stegoceras (steh-GOS-er-us) dinosaur
lived on rocky mountainsides.

Now look carefully and you will find
5 things different. Circle them.

Shunosaurus (SHOO-no-SORE-us) is standing on its two back feet to eat, but it walked on all four feet.

Find the 5 differences in this picture and circle them.

Brachiosaurus (brak-ee-oh-SORE-us) was one of the
longest and heaviest of the dinosaurs.

Find and circle the 5 things that have
changed in the picture.

Iguanadon (ig-WAN-oh-don) had a spiky thumb
that it used to protect itself.

There are 4 differences between this picture
and the other. Find and circle them.

23

Plesiosaur (PLEE-zee-oh-SORE) had paddlelike
arms and legs that it used to swim.

Find and circle the 6 differences between this picture
and the one opposite.

The Triassic (try-YASS-ick) turtle is not very
different from turtles living today.

Look carefully at the picture of the Triassic turtle.
Circle the 5 things that are different.

The Raptor (RAP-tore) had curved claws
and very sharp teeth.

This picture of the Raptor is different.
Circle the 7 differences.

The flying Pterodactyl (TER-oh-DAK-til)
caught fish for its meals.

Find and circle the 5 differences in
this picture of Pterodactyl.

Stegosaurus (STEG-oh-SORE-us)
had bony plates on its back and tail.

Here is Stegosaurus, but 6 things are different.
Find and circle them.

Euparkeria (you-park-ERR-ee-yuh) walked
on all four legs but ran on two.

Find and circle the 5 differences
in this picture of Euparkeria.

35

Enormous Camarasaurus (kam-are-ah-SORE-us)
was about 60 feet long.

Find the 5 differences between this picture
of Camarasaurus and the other.

Placodus (PLAK-oh-diss) watches a
baby dinosaur hatch out of its egg.

Now there are 5 things different
in the picture. Circle them all.

Pliosaur (PLEE-oh-sore) was a short-necked
sea creature with sharp teeth.

In this picture of Pliosaur, 6 things are different.
Find all 6 and circle them.

Parasaurolophus (par-a-SORE-oh-LOAF-us)
ate leaves, fruits, and plants.

There are 5 differences in this picture.
Find and circle them.

Teleosaurus (TELL-ee-oh-SORE-us) was an
early relative of the crocodile.

Find and circle the 5 differences between
this picture and the other.

Long-necked Barosaurus (bar-oh-SORE-us)
enjoyed nibbling leaves from treetops.

This picture contains 5 things that are
different. Find and circle them.

Hadrosaurus (HAD-row-SORE-us)
was a dinosaur with a large, toothless beak.

There are 5 differences between this
picture and the other. Find and circle them.

Carnotaurus (KAR-no-TORE-us) had two horns
on its head and a row of scales on its back.

Look carefully at this picture. Circle the 5 things that
make it different from the other picture.

Dimetrodon (DYE-meh-TRO-don)
had a kind of "sail" on its back.

Find and circle the 5 ways that this
picture is different from the other one.

Thecodontosaurus (THEEK-oh-DON-toe-SORE-us)
may have been the first dinosaur to eat
both plants and animals.

Find and circle the 6 differences
between this picture and the other.

Tiny Nanosaurus (nan-oh-SORE-us)
was under 6 feet long.

Look carefully at this picture. Find and circle the
6 differences between this picture and the other.

57

Solutions

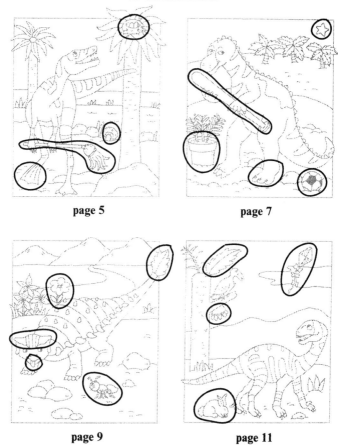

page 5

page 7

page 9

page 11

page 13

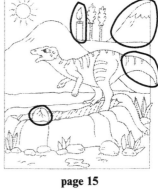

page 15

page 17

page 19

page 21

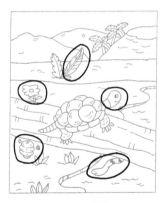

page 23

page 25

page 27

page 29

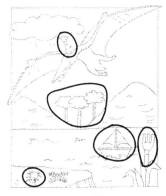

page 31

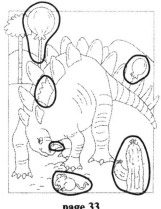

page 33

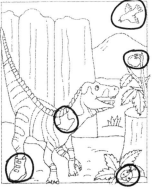

page 35

page 37

page 39

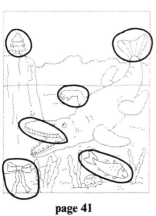

page 41

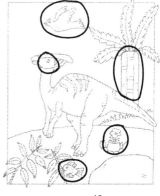

page 43

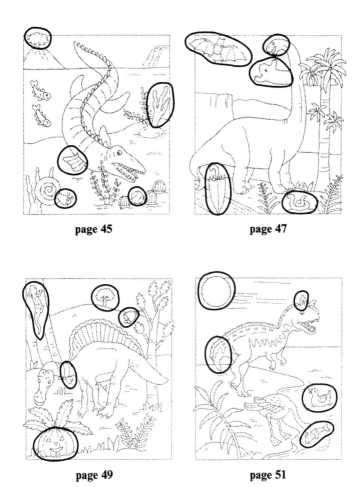

page 45

page 47

page 49

page 51

page 53

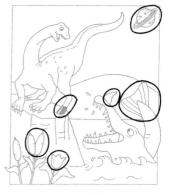

page 55

page 57